LEARNING FOR ALL

UNIT 13

FURTHER AND HIGHER

Prepared for the course team by
Jenny Corbett

The Open University

E242 COURSE READERS

There are two course readers associated with E242; they are:

BOOTH, T., SWANN, W., MASTERTON, M. and POTTS, P. (eds) (1992) *Learning for All 1: curricula for diversity in education*, London, Routledge (**Reader 1**).

BOOTH, T., SWANN, W., MASTERTON, M. and POTTS, P. (eds) (1992) *Learning for All 2: policies for diversity in education*, London, Routledge (**Reader 2**).

TELEVISION PROGRAMMES AND AUDIO-CASSETTES

There are eight TV programmes and three audio-cassettes associated with E242. They are closely integrated into the unit texts and there are no separate TV or cassette notes. However, further information about them may be obtained by writing to Open University Educational Enterprises Ltd, 12 Cofferidge Close, Stony Stratford, Milton Keynes MK11 1BY.

Cover illustration shows a detail from 'Midsummer Common' by Dorothy Bordass.

The Open University, Walton Hall, Milton Keynes MK7 6AA

First published 1992. Reprinted 1994

Designed by the Graphic Design Group of The Open University

Typeset by The Open University

Printed in the United Kingdom by Page Bros (Norwich) Ltd

ISBN 0 7492 6113 7

This unit forms part of an Open University course; the complete list of units is printed at the end of this book. If you have not enrolled on the course and would like to buy this or other Open University material, please write to Open University Educational Enterprises Ltd, 12 Cofferidge Close, Stony Stratford MK11 1BY, United Kingdom. If you wish to enquire about enrolling as an Open University student, please write to the Admissions Office, The Open University, PO Box 48, Walton Hall, Milton Keynes MK7 6AB, United Kingdom.

CONTENTS

1 INTRODUCTION

1.1   This unit explores what happens to the school students you have been introduced to in earlier units. What becomes of those who grow disenchanted with school and leave at the first opportunity, perhaps truanting over the last two years? What happens to pupils with sensory or physical disabilities who were members of mainstream secondary schools? What are the choices open to these leavers for a life after school?

1.2   A major theme of this unit is the idea of transition, of moving from school and adolescence to training, employment, further education and adult life. The choices which are available are constrained by political and economic factors, by regional variations in the pattern of opportunities and by the enduring discrimination that people experience because of their class, gender, race or disability.

1.3   A second theme is the extent to which young people with learning difficulties or disabilities are or should be integrated, on leaving school, into mainstream further and higher education, into open employment and into the ordinary life of their communities.

1.4   The unit has three main sections. Section 2 explores the concept of transition in relation to these young people, looking at a European perspective and also at the way in which inequalities of opportunity can further complicate an already difficult stage of life.

1.5   Section 3, the longest in the unit, focuses on the transition from school to further or higher education. After describing the developments that took place in the 1980s, specialized further education is discussed, in relation both to residential provision and to special school–mainstream further education (FE) college link courses. Moves towards more integrated further education are then discussed, from the perspectives of students on a particular course and lecturers responsible for developing whole-college policies. The section concludes with a detailed look at policy and provision in the London borough of Haringey and you will be asked to watch and discuss the related television programme *Linking into the Future*.

1.6   Section 4 looks at the transitions from school to vocational training, to employment or unemployment and at the way in which school curricula for many fourteen- to sixteen-year-olds have increasingly been work-oriented.

RESOURCES FOR THIS UNIT

1.7   It will take up to three weeks for you to study this unit, but depending on your progress through the previous units and your particular interests you may wish to devote more or less time to the material presented here. In addition to the unit text you will be studying the following additional material:

2 PERSPECTIVES ON TRANSITION

2.1 This section consists of a sequence of three activities. In the first you are asked to reflect on what it means to be 'adult'. In the second you are asked to read and discuss the provision that is made across Europe for students with learning difficulties or disabilities and in the third you are asked to consider how discrimination on the grounds of race, class, gender or disability can impose additional disadvantages.

Activity 1 Transition to adult life

What does it mean to be 'adult'? What, in our society in the 1990s, are the consequences of not being adult, as it is conventionally defined? How important is it to be able to exercise some personal choice rather than to conform to the stereotype of economic independence? How far are people allowed to be 'adult' if they require support to cope with the responsibilities that may follow from making active choices?

Read the following brief descriptions of four people's everyday lives and consider the following questions.

- What range of choices have Peter, Jacquie, Jimmy and Clare been able to make to secure a way of life that suits them?

- Would you say that they are leading 'adult lives'?

- How much is your response to the last question determined by the circumstances of their daily lives, rather than by the extent to which these four people have actively chosen them?

- Do you want to be an 'adult' all the time?

Peter

Peter is now twenty-one. He went on from a special school to a special two-year college course and, from there, on to a Youth Training (YT) programme. In some areas of the country he would have been guided towards the social education centre and sheltered employment. Instead, he is supported in a work placement on which he works for four days a week in the kitchen of a local hotel and spends the fifth day on a college catering course. In the hotel kitchen he prepares vegetables, washes up and bakes cakes and biscuits. Peter had been sacked from two previous work placements for his lack of concentration and unpredictability. Without the active and sustained support of the programme's staff and his sympathetic new employers, Peter would not have the degree of control over his life that he now enjoys. He hopes to continue working in the hotel when his training period is completed.

Not only is Peter preparing for work, he has recently moved out of his parents' home into a house which he shares with two other young men. They have daily support but are expected to share household chores. Peter is an active member of the village community in which he lives, for example taking part in the musicals which are sometimes presented.

However, Peter still visits his parents every weekend and wants their regular help and guidance.

It is also true that sometimes Peter does not want to participate in the social life of his new home nor to co-operate at work. Like most people, Peter feels more ready to accept responsibilities on some days than on others.

Peter has Down's syndrome.

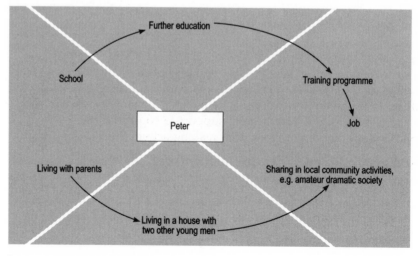

Peter: transition to adult life.

Jacquie

Jacquie left her comprehensive school at the end of her third year. She looked for work telling employers that she was sixteen when she was in fact fourteen. She got a job working in a shoe shop but was unhappy there. The manager sexually harassed her and she left. What Jacquie really wanted to do was to work with children but she thought that, with no formal qualifications, she had no chance of doing this. She decided to try a YT programme. Her chosen option was community care, which involved caring for young children or old people. Jacquie enjoyed this very much, accepting the responsibilities that went with the work placement. Whereas she had truanted from school, she now felt an obligation to be reliable in her work for the YT course. There was pressure from her unemployed parents for Jacquie to give up the training in order to earn more money but Jacquie persuaded them that her training was worthwhile as it could lead to a career as a nanny or a nursery nurse. Her ambition, at sixteen, is to become a nanny in the USA.

Jacquie, like Peter, was seen as having 'special educational needs' at school. Like Peter, her expectations and hopes for the future involve extending the interests which she has just recently developed. They are both discovering what they might like to do in the future, how they can go about achieving their ambitions and who can offer them support.

Jimmy

Jimmy is thirty-two and on four days a week he attends a social education centre. There, he does recreational activities and occasional light industrial work for local firms. He goes to the local college of further education one day a week to do a cookery class and a computer class. He plays football for his club, which is designed to cater largely for adults with learning difficulties. On Sundays he attends the church at the end of the street and sings with the choir. In the weekday evenings and on Saturdays he spends a good deal of time walking up and down outside the local parade of shops, chatting with neighbours who know him, telling them about his experiences on the football pitch, his trips out on residential excursions with the centre and his arguments with friends. Jimmy lives with his mother and, from his frequent references to her in conversation, she is clearly still a considerable influence on his thinking.

Clare

Clare is thirty-three and attends a day centre every day of the week except Friday. There, she edits a magazine for local disabled people which has had a wide circulation beyond the immediate locality. As Clare is only able to control her left foot, she uses this foot to work a computer on which she writes poems, articles and letters to correspondents. She lives with her parents and her dog and has chosen not to go into a centre of independent living, as she is very close to her family and enjoys her life with them.

Like Jimmy, Clare is living in the community in which she grew up and like him she is still at home with her parents. They both attend day centres and are involved in a social life both there and in their neighbourhood. Neither of them is employed but both receive benefits.

2.2   Choices for Peter, Jacquie, Jimmy and Clare included continuing to live with parents or moving into alternative accommodation; taking a 'dead-end' job or choosing training; attending college courses for students 'with special needs' or moving into mainstream courses. It would be naive to assume that the choices offered are necessarily real. Often it is a case of having to compromise, take what is available and cope with less than satisfactory options.

2.3   One colleague told me that she recognized her transition to adulthood the first time that she left her parent's home without feeling a pang of regret and slight panic. At this stage she had been married for some years and had two children! Yet she still found difficulty in accepting her adult role as parent and found it comforting to be parented again. I find this a useful example, both for its candour and the way in which it indicates that transitions develop in stages, subtle and unpredictable. None of us suddenly becomes perceptibly adult. Responsibilities creep up on us. We can all be contradictory in our adulthood, accepting certain responsibilities while avoiding others. Fortunately for most of us, we are rarely assessed on the quality of our domestic lives but on our capacity to cope with social interchange and the demands of a sophisticated world. It is ironic that those who practise public adulthood successfully can avoid scrutiny of their possibly incompetent private lives, whilst the most disadvantaged and disabled adults have to endure lifelong intrusion and guidance in the most intimate areas of their daily life. The very existence of courses on *Transition to Adulthood* (Hutchinson and Tennyson, 1986) for young people with disabilities, but not for all adolescents following the National Curriculum, illustrates that transition is perceived as a process experienced automatically by the majority yet which for the minority needs to be rehearsed.

2.4   It may be easy to assume that living with parents indicates a childish dependence, but it may also be the case that it indicates a recognition that greater independence and personal satisfaction can follow from the availability of domestic support. It may appear immature to reject the adult status conferred by wage-earning, whatever the actual job, but this rejection may also reflect an awareness of the right to an occupation that matches one's abilities and interests. It may seem like a refusal to grow up if a young man or woman enrols at a residential special college, but it may also represent a significant move away from home and towards a network of social relationships with other young people.

2.5   Whether or not we see people as 'adult' can depend too much on the superficial circumstances of their daily lives and too little on the less obvious extent to which some autonomous decision has been made, the extent to which living at home means independence for some people just as living away from home means independence for others. It depends upon your perspective. Many people's grown-up lives may not fit a narrow definition of what it means to be 'adult', and a narrow definition may obscure the fact that it may be neither possible nor desirable to be 'adult' all the time.

2.6   The idea of transition to an adult life is a complex and contradictory one. We may continue to enter new phases of adulthood and self-identity at a number of different, unpredictable times in our lives. A transition, in the sense of a period of fruitful growth, can occur at any stage.

Activity 2   An international perspective

Now read 'An international perspective on transition' by John Fish (Reader 2, Chapter 10).

As you read, consider the following questions:

- How does John Fish define 'transition' and what it means to be 'adult'?

- What reasons does he give for the increased attention paid to the transition of young people with learning difficulties or disabilities as they leave school and go on to further education, training, employment, unemployment or community living?

- What strategies does John Fish outline for making transitional experiences easier and what examples of good practice does he give?

- What obstacles does he describe and how do you think they might be overcome?

2.7   John Fish supports a view of transition as both 'a phase and a process', involving moving from childhood, adolescence and dependence to an adulthood which is characterized by independence and wage-earning. Later in the chapter, he acknowledges that personal experience of this transition can be 'confused'.

2.8   The transition of young people from school to life after school has attracted increased attention during the 1980s and early 1990s because of a number of factors, for example: the high rate of youth unemployment; demographic trends which have resulted in more people retiring from than entering employment; the demands of technology at work; and the effects of recent legislation, such as the Education Reform Act (1988) which has a major section covering arrangements for students in post-compulsory education. For Fish, the transition from adolescence to adulthood is one of the most important transitions we have to experience during our lives and he sees this time as crucially important for young people with disabilities or learning difficulties.

2.9   It is not altogether clear that Fish sees the situation as wholly a bad thing because he also describes how, in a context in which the numbers of young people leaving school are noticeably falling, there may in fact be increased opportunities for all young people. However, in 1992, at the time this unit was being written, youth unemployment and competition for jobs was still increasing.

2.10   Fish stresses the value of inter-agency collaboration but he acknowledges that, even if services were well co-ordinated and working together towards clear aims, this might be rejected by young people themselves who could see the support services usurping their own personal autonomy and control. However, it remains a problem that many health and social services are provided, through the school system, for young people up to the age of sixteen and then stop. For transition to a meaningful life in the community, whether it be from school, college or a long-stay hospital, there has to be a support network to enable realistic choices to be made.

2.11   Fish notes that the *Kurator* in Denmark offers an exceptional level of continuity. The *Kurator* deals with the following:

(a) *School circumstances.* Choice of subjects, vocational orientation, work experience and placement, continued education, educational grants, youth schools.

(b) *Further education and training.* Continuation schools, evening schools, home economic schools, vocational schools, apprenticeships, basic vocational education and semi-skilled workers training schools.

(c) *Working conditions.* Choice of career, applications, references, salaries and conditions, careers officers, employers, trade unions and legislation.

(d) *Personal matters.* Disability, the home environment, economics, leisure time, accidents, military service, social security, public offices and services and social welfare.

(Boyd Kjellen, 1991, p. 23)

2.12   The overall role of the *Kurator* is that of a guide and support in all aspects of transition. This means that there is one source of continuity, managing the complex network of services. In a recent assessment of community services, Baldwin and Hattersley (1991) promote an interdisciplinary approach, which includes carers, staff, friends and family members, working together with the service user to agree upon a single programme plan.

2.13   Fish illustrates the contradictory elements within services to support transition when he indicates that training for independence and employment may exist alongside a system which offers benefits for disabled people as long as they remain dependent and have an 'unemployable' status. The temptation to accept dependency is powerful, especially if becoming more independent involves struggling with tedious domestic chores. The benefits system still promulgates a deficiency model, in which not being able to find employment is seen as due to inadequacies of disabled individuals, and not to the inequities of the labour market. In the Disability Living Allowance and Disability Working Allowance Act (1991), it is stated that people are entitled to a disability working allowance if they have a physical or mental disability which puts them at a disadvantage in getting a job. It is the disability which is seen as the problem. The 'disadvantages' of prejudice, low expectations and inadequate educational opportunities are not considered.

2.14   Fish suggests that the transfer of power from parents and professionals to individuals with disabilities can be problematic. This is a complex and contentious area. In further education for students with learning difficulties, parents have been seen as key elements in helping to generalize the social skills which their sons and daughters learn in college. Yet if lecturers are to help the young people to make their own choices, there needs to be the same minimal level of parental consultation that there is with parents of other students. Sometimes parents resist the extent of independent decision-making which is being encouraged in students and this can lead to conflict between parents and staff.

2.15   But what about the young people themselves? Their voices and views are absent from the discussion.

Activity 3   Transition and equality of opportunity

Now read 'The rhetoric and reality of transition to adult life', by Jenny Corbett and Len Barton (Reader 2, Chapter 11).

As you read, consider the following questions:

*   How are the concepts 'transition' and 'adult' defined? What criticisms are made of the way in which these concepts are commonly used? Compare the approach to transition taken in this chapter with that adopted by John Fish.

*   How many rhetoric–reality gaps are referred to and what are they?

2.16   Transition to adult life should involve increased participation in employment, leisure activities and social integration. But there are many kinds of adulthood and a wider range of transitional experiences for young people than is often recognized. For example, the transition to homelessness may be ignored, despite its increasing frequency among young people. The concept of transition to adult life is 'complex and contentious', a political issue which needs to be set within a critique of the social context of young people's lives. Fish's narrow and undifferentiated view fails to acknowledge the influence of class, race and gender, as well as that of varying abilities, on the experience of transition. The resulting inequalities have to be addressed if all young people are to experience a positive transition to adult life.

2.17 Educators frequently omit both discussing how the complexities of the social world influence the lives of their students and recognizing that this happens in ways that do not promote equality of opportunity but which reflect wider discriminations against the least powerful groups.

2.18 Parents who are affluent and well-educated are able to offer more opportunities to their adolescent sons and daughters, so that their experience of transition is eased. Class, gender and skin-colour factors still affect the extent of choice. One YT provision, for example, which I visited in 1991, had a sewing section exclusively for young women aged sixteen to eighteen, in which working-class 'girls' were being prepared for work in local sewing factories. Many of these young people were perceived as having 'moderate learning difficulties'; but it was their class and gender which were the main inhibitors of choice. Another workshop (Corbett, 1990a) had about an 85 per cent black clientele. In this provision, staff felt that they had to make the young people presentable to employers by ensuring their compliance and reliability, as they knew there was likely to be initial hostility and prejudice. While some of the young people on this programme were described as having 'moderate learning difficulties', they also had to cope with racism. Other young people have to struggle with extreme poverty during this period of transition (Wilkinson, 1990). These variations will inevitably influence the extent to which their choices are realizable.

2.19 Four rhetoric–reality gaps are discussed in the chapter: that between a rhetoric of 'work' and a reality of 'no choice'; that between a rhetoric of 'choice' and a reality of economic and cultural 'devaluation'; that between a rhetoric of 'autonomy' and a reality of parental control and 'no opportunities'; and that between a rhetoric of 'empowerment' and a reality of the 'invasion of privacy'. For many young people, the experience of transition is one of oppression rather than liberation.

3 TRANSITION TO FURTHER AND HIGHER EDUCATION

3.1 This section looks at the range of post-school educational provision for young people with disabilities or learning difficulties. It is mainly concerned with further education (FE), rather than higher education (HE). The Education Reform Act (1988) included a major section on 16–19 education, the first time that a commitment to this age-group had been confirmed by legislation. The potential range of options for young people is wide and complicated, though in practice what is available to students locally may be quite limited and not necessarily well suited to their capacities, interests or hopes for the future.

3.2   After a brief look at higher education, I set the scene for further education with a look at the changes of the 1980s and an outline of national policy in the early 1990s. This is followed by a discussion of specialized further education which focuses on residential college courses and on special school–mainstream college link courses. Attempts to develop a whole-college approach to providing for students with widely varying abilities and interests within the mainstream are discussed from the perspectives of both students and lecturers. The section concludes with a detailed look at integrated provision in the north London borough of Haringey.

3.3   In as much as many courses provided in FE colleges are vocational or may be directly connected to particular training courses, there is overlap between issues relevant to this section and those relating to the next, on training and work. In an attempt to simplify the narrative, I have included material on vocational curricula in schools and training courses at FE colleges in Section 4. Some overlap remains, however, particularly in relation to the Haringey case study.

HIGHER EDUCATION

3.4   Some students with disabilities or learning difficulties move on to higher education. Yet they remain a small minority. Compared to integration in further education, integration in higher education is at a very superficial level. Skill (the National Bureau for Students with Disabilities) was originally created with a focus on higher education, but it is now predominantly concerned with FE. Why has HE presented barriers to access?

3.5   The Open University offers the most extensive services to such students and caters for the highest numbers nationally, with between 3,000 and 4,000 disabled students. This provision includes weekend residential courses to prepare students who experience visual and hearing difficulties for university study and the use of interpreters and assistants at summer schools. It also involves specialist support and guidance in study skills and help for those students who have difficulties with reading and writing for their assignments. Course units are routinely read on audio-cassettes for blind students. Many HE institutions now offer services for disabled students as part of their equal opportunities policies, but there are still many campuses which remain inaccessible (Hurst, 1990).

3.6   Where universities and polytechnics offer specially adapted accommodation for disabled students, this can create difficulties as well as solving them. It forces a degree of segregation and can equate 'disability' with 'sickness' if located, for example, in the student health centre (Hurst, 1990). Coping with campus life can be demanding for disabled students but even reaching that stage is often fraught with obstacles. Hurst (1990) records the problems faced by disabled applicants who find themselves rejected without interview because the institution is inaccessible. Often caution and misunderstandings between HE staff and disabled applicants inhibit their proceeding further.

3.7   In order to improve access and encourage disabled applicants, Lancashire Polytechnic has created a 'named person' to be responsible for managing liaison with disabled students' enquiries. Once students are part of the polytechnic community, they are invited to regular meetings to air issues of mutual concern. Staff are helped to modify their methods of student assessment. Such productive approaches have been disseminated to other HE institutions throughout the United Kingdom, and responsive services for students with disabilities are increasingly viewed as an integral part of ensuring equality of opportunity.

3.8   In the Polytechnic of East London, support is viewed as part of an equal opportunities policy. The Dean of Equal Opportunities arranged a series of awareness-raising events in the institution, in the academic year 1990/91, which included feminist debates and entertainments, race-awareness and cultural events to celebrate the diverse community of the polytechnic, and events related to disability issues. These included a wheelchair race around areas of the campus and a performance by a group of professional actors with learning difficulties who attended a social educational centre.

3.9   For some students at the polytechnic, their disability is only one of many problems they face. One Afro-Caribbean woman, for example, had to cope with a degree of racial and sexual harassment, poor housing, desperate economic need and loneliness in addition to her disabling condition of deteriorating vision and hearing. The polytechnic can offer some basic aids, like tape-recorders and transcribers, but it is complicated to arrange the level of social service support and benefits which are required and some aspects of this student's difficulties remained unresolved.

3.10   In many respects, the Polytechnic of East London probably typifies an institution of higher education which has a high level of awareness of equal opportunities but can only address some of the issues. Services like the study skills centre provide teaching support and guidance for those students experiencing difficulties in their learning. Reasonable access enables students in wheelchairs to attend courses. The counselling service accommodates students with a range of anxieties. Yet there are always issues which require complex and sustained support beyond the capacity of the institution.

3.11   Developments in higher education in the early 1990s, including the blurring of the traditional distinction between polytechnics and universities, the growth of modular courses and accreditation of previous learning experiences, are leading to a more 'student-centred' approach. Methods of course delivery and design are being developed to incorporate a range of styles and alternative assessment procedures devised to help all students, especially those coming into higher education after a long gap between their compulsory schooling and return to learning. Learners in higher education have many diverse needs. The notion of 'special educational need' becomes particularly nebulous in this context. Mature students often feel a need for help with long-forgotten essay writing. Some students come to higher education with their earlier diagnosis of 'dyslexia', asking for the help they feel they require. Students with sensory and physical disabilities may need specific aids or an interpreter or care attendant. What constitutes 'need' relates directly to the skills and outcomes associated with higher education. Yet disabled students are likely to face new barriers when they leave to seek employment or vocational training, barriers created by prejudice and misunderstanding.

FURTHER EDUCATION

3.12   Although the system of further education in the United Kingdom has evolved and expanded during the 1980s and 1990s, it is important to realize that post-school educational provision generally remains a contentious area.

Changes in the 1980s

3.13   Colleges of further education were originally designed to be *open* institutions, responsive to local developments and providing:

> full-time and part-time education for persons over compulsory school age; and leisure time occupation in such organized cultural, training and recreative activities as are suited to their requirements for any persons over compulsory school age who are able and willing to profit by the facilities provided for that purpose.
>
> (Education Act, 1944, Section 41)

3.14   Colleges offer a diverse range of educational and vocational training – from A-levels to hairdressing, business studies to plumbing, engineering to basic skills – and were intended to be responsive to changing local needs, both educational and economic. In contrast to schools, there is no compulsion to attend and courses have to be seen to be viable, with student–staff ratios of at least 12 to 1.

An expanding system

3.15   The 1980s saw a rapid expansion of FE provision for students with disabilities or learning difficulties (Stowell, 1987). Provision was not spread evenly, however, as some regions of Britain developed facilities much earlier than others (Bradley and Hegarty, 1981). This created inequities; for example, some students who use wheelchairs were forced to attend a college far from their immediate locality, as it was the only one in the region which was 'accessible'.

Integration into the mainstream

3.16   The integration of students with disabilities or other difficulties has always occurred on a modest scale, such as when the students concerned made minimal demands on physical resourcing or on curricular provision. Some colleges are still operating at this low level of commitment. The more recent inclusion of students with severe learning difficulties has been accompanied by the evolution of a separate special curriculum in many FE colleges.

Curriculum development

3.17   A rapidly expanding group of students in further education for whom there was no appropriate curriculum within the traditional range of courses were those who had been identified as having 'moderate learning difficulties'. *From Coping to Confidence* (Bradley, 1985), a staff-development package funded by the Department of Education and Science, presented a teaching framework designed for use with this group of students.

3.18   Hutchinson and Tennyson (1986), in their curriculum document *Transition to Adulthood*, were responding to the evident needs of students with complex physical and additional disabilities who were attending North Nottinghamshire College. As one of those colleges which had made early provision for students with disabilities, offering access from the 1960s onwards, North Nottinghamshire College has developed into a centre of excellence in the area of curriculum development for students with 'special educational needs'. While this means it can offer both good physical access and curricular flexibility, it also confirms national inequities. The establishment in certain FE colleges of a reputation for supporting students with disabilities has allowed other colleges to abdicate their responsibility and has inevitably restricted student choice. A special section has developed in further education. Not only are specific colleges selected for certain disabilities but also the transfer of special school staff and structures has created special units inside colleges.

3.19   The dissemination of a curriculum framework in *New Directions* (Dee, 1988) reflected concern to respond to the needs of students with severe learning difficulties coming into mainstream colleges from special schools. The range of teaching strategies and curricular ideas offered derive from a commitment to normalization, self-advocacy and entitlement. Normalization (see also Unit 10) refers to the belief that the common humanity of people should be stressed rather than their exceptional differences. It follows therefore that everyone shares an equal right to participation in the ordinary life of their communities. Self-advocacy refers to the exercise of autonomy by those people whose voices and wishes have been suppressed in the past. Entitlement has a more specifically educational meaning in the 1990s and refers to the right of all students to access to the full range of curricular activities and to the subsequent range of optional choices at the end of their educational career.

3.20 Faraday and Harris (1989) have introduced a learner-centred approach in *Learning Support*, a staff-development pack supported by the Training Agency. In this, the emphasis is on negotiated learning systems in which students with difficulties in learning are supported in mainstream or special groups by an analysis of their individual needs and their own perceived requirements. This reflects a move towards enabling all learners to share in negotiating their learning experiences, which becomes a whole-college responsibility, no longer the province of the 'special needs' department.

3.21 Under the terms of the 1988 Education Reform Act, curriculum entitlement is seen to be concerned with obligations and rights in which providers are expected to enable learners to gain access to the resources they require (Further Education Unit, 1989). The National Union of Teachers (NUT, 1990) reflects upon the potential impact of the 1988 Education Act on future provision for post-sixteen students:

> The 1988 Education Act appears to plug the loophole in the 1944 Education Act by making it the duty of every LEA to 'secure ... adequate facilities in FE colleges' and to 'have regard to the requirements of persons over compulsory school age who have learning difficulties'. However, in conferring power to LEAs to 'do anything which appears ... necessary' for students with [special educational needs], the 1988 Act allows local authorities to retain the element of choice as to the extent to which they use those powers. Nevertheless, the 1988 Act has allowed, for example, Sutton LEA in co-operation with its Social Services Department, to assess the special educational needs of its post-16 students and give them statements of provision in its FE colleges. Such statements, where the right courses are not available, may define specific programmes of provision for the individual student. Sutton has also decided to allow the full assessment and statement process to continue up until the age of 30.
>
> (NUT, 1990, pp. 2–3)

This example illustrates the impact of national policy on local policy and, in its turn, on institutional policy and practice.

3.22 Looking at the powers now given to college governing bodies, Skill recommends that:

> *every* college should have at least one governor with experience of special educational needs, since the community which every college serves will include people with special educational needs.
>
> (Skill, 1991a, p. 4)

Skill notes that some colleges have a 'special needs' representative while others do not, although most colleges are providing awareness training for governors. As Section 140 of the Education Reform Act 1988 requires local authorities to prepare schemes for planning and delegating responsibilities for further education, Skill recommends the inclusion of a declaration of commitment to meeting the full range of educational needs.

3.23 Skill also recommends the inclusion, in the planning process within each authority, of an inter-departmental and inter-agency process for establishing the likely numbers of students with disabilities or learning difficulties. For example, area health authorities already have a system for joint planning with social services and education authorities which, in most cases, could be more fully exploited (Skill, 1991a, p. 6).

3.24 The government White Paper, *Education and Training for the 21st Century* (DES, 1991), created something of a stir. Brenchley, writing in the *Times Educational Supplement* (5 July 1991), reflects that the government appeared to have contradicted its commitment to local authority delegation within the 1988 Education Reform Act:

> Something dramatic must have happened to change the LEA's role and contribution so much so quickly ... The reason for the new funding proposals has nothing at all to do with education and training, and everything to do with the politics of poll tax and local government reform.
>
> (Brenchley, 1991, p. 16)

3.25 The leader comment in the same edition illustrates the inequalities within the White Paper which disadvantage adults with disabilities or learning difficulties. The White Paper devotes only 360 words to the 3.4 million adults in voluntary part-time education. These 'leisure interest' courses were threatened. This would have had severe implications for those adults recently moved from institutions into the community, for whom they offer sources of stimulus and social interchange. As the *TES* leader states:

> The white paper's exclusive list ignores where many of the over-19s entering some kind of adult education actually begin.
>
> They may be deeply hostile to all forms of education, thanks to their own schooling – particularly if they ended it illiterate or innumerate. They may have lost all self-confidence, because of illness, or long-term unemployment, or even domesticity.
>
> For them, the distinction between 'leisure interest' and 'vocational' courses is meaningless. The great thing is that they should be encouraged back to education in some form, and that all courses should aim to build their self-confidence and personal skills.
>
> (*TES*, 5 July 1991, p. 17)

3.26 In a discussion on the implications of the White Paper for students with disabilities or learning difficulties, Skill (1991b) notes:

> Skill wishes to see a guarantee that adults will receive educational opportunities on request. Skill also seeks a clear recognition of the need for a wide range of adult opportunities. For example, an indication that basic skills is not just literacy and numeracy ... but includes other provision that enhances self-advocacy and

self-confidence and may well be the essential link to vocational courses and work (e.g. lip-reading classes).

(Skill, 1991b, p. 4)

Such a guarantee, however, seems unlikely to be given credence in a White Paper which focuses upon outcomes rather than needs.

3.27   The White Paper makes further recommendations relating to quality, qualifications and administration. Skill seeks assurance that developments which have been beneficial for students with disabilities and learning difficulties are not to be threatened by changes in practice. Skill asks for proposed new diplomas and vocational qualifications to be made accessible in the way TVEI and CPVE courses have been (see Section 4); for 'performance indicators' to be based on progress being made, if they are not to become barriers to equality of opportunity; for the designated role of Her Majesty's Inspectorate with national responsibility for further and higher education to continue, as it has always been a source of support and innovation in this area; finally, for continued funding for staff development.

3.28   Other legislative changes have implications for the transition from school to college or higher education or training, which the 1991 White Paper may influence. These include community care arrangements, implementation of Sections 5 and 6 of the Disabled Persons' Act (1988) and the Children Act (1989). The continuity of transition between education authority, college and social services provision, with which these Acts are concerned, is particularly important for young people with complex disabilities.

3.29   Further education is currently experiencing dramatic changes. Yet, in a sense, it has always been a volatile sector which thrives on short-term responsiveness. Part of its recent history has included the expansion of provision for students with special educational needs. While these students have become an established part of the FE community, they remain a vulnerable minority especially in a market-led and cost-cutting climate.

SEGREGATED FURTHER EDUCATION

3.30   When examining FE provision overall, it is important to note what in fact constitutes the special education sector in further education. You have just read about the potentially segregating effects that the unusually progressive practice of a particular college may have upon the experience of its students. This was an adverse consequence of the early development of appropriate and accessible curricula at North Nottinghamshire College. But whereas residential special schools form only a small proportion of the total number of special schools in the United Kingdom, residential special colleges form the major source of special further education.

Residential provision

3.31   Residential colleges are often run by voluntary sector organizations like the Spastics Society or the Royal National Institutes for the Blind or the Deaf, or are run by communities based on religious foundations. In their compendium of national provision, Lillystone and Summerson (1987) illustrate the wide range of needs which are included, the very restricted numbers usually catered for and the curricular focus on training for 'independence'. One small centre, for twenty 'emotionally disturbed young people' aged sixteen to nineteen, for example, was said to help them to become better equipped to cope in the community with its emphasis on a family atmosphere, love and security. You may wonder how such a small, specialized and segregated community could ever hope to achieve its aim of readjustment. Also, does a protective family atmosphere adequately prepare young people for the harsher realities of an uncaring and sometimes hostile community?

3.32   In her chapter 'Integration policy in Newham, 1986–90' (Reader 2, Chapter 32), Linda Jordan states that the numbers of Newham children and young people receiving special education in residential schools had been cut from 100 to 25 in four years. This represents a huge saving for Newham because residential places are very expensive. When I discussed FE provision for students in another London borough in June 1991, the special needs advisory teacher told me that there was still a high demand for residential special colleges as current borough provision was seen as inadequate. This borough, like Newham, had to address the flexibility and receptiveness of its FE sector as it could no longer afford to keep funding students for what is now perceived as an undesirable form of provision. Going away to residential college at sixteen first uproots students from their localities and then returns them at nineteen, often with little chance of employment, independent housing or day-time facilities. It will be interesting to see if Newham's new fully accessible sixth-form college, to be opened in September 1992, will mean that no student in this locality need go away for residential further education in the future.

3.33   Why are students sent to residential special colleges if the cost is so high and the disadvantages evident? While the students whose disabilities or learning difficulties are seen as manageable in mainstream FE are likely to be accepted in local colleges, those who present more complex difficulties are not. I studied the curriculum and ethos of one residential college, which accepts students from a wide geographical area and caters for about fifty young people aged 16–19 (Corbett, 1989a, 1991a). The students may have physical disabilities as well as learning difficulties and often they experience additional emotional problems. It seems to be the complexity of their perceived needs that has brought them into residential provision. However, when talking to tearful and homesick sixteen-year-old students there, I thought of my own son, who was sixteen at that time, and how difficult he would find such a transfer. The very environment of a residential college, with minimal space for privacy and an enforced daily regime, would be more likely to promote emotional instability in teenagers who might already have low self-esteem.

Communicating needs: students in a residential special college

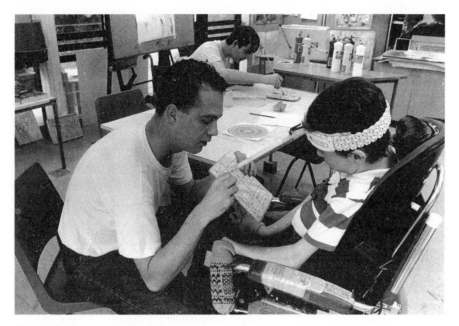

Communicating with the tutor in an art class.

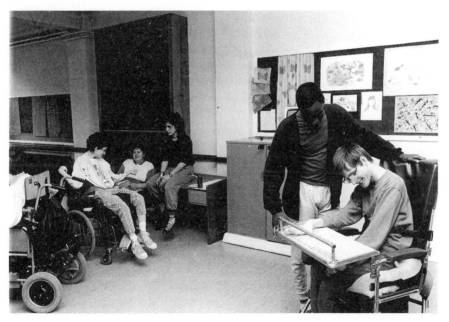

Communicating with care staff in the lunch break.

Curricula in residential settings

3.34   In examining the curriculum prevalent in some special colleges, bear in mind the issues which were raised in Unit 8/9. These included a concern not to impose definitions of 'normality' on those children being taught. The young people described by Hewett and Nind (Reader 1, Chapter 18) were not children, however, but young adults. They had been taught by a behavioural approach which was later abandoned. The curriculum within the special college that I studied also underwent profound changes. It moved from a traditional subject-based approach to an emphasis on student empowerment, choice and control, with the students at the centre of the curriculum, defining their needs and priorities. Such a development mirrors that described by Hewett and Nind. It is about encouraging students to take the initiative and about expecting staff to respect this.

3.35   However, caution is needed to avoid creating an artificial 'normality'. Hewett and Nind's mother–baby interaction for student learners could be questioned: might it be oppressive to treat these adults like babies? The curriculum I observed at the special college focused on domestic skills, shopping, laundry and home management as well as self-expression and assertion. When most other teenagers actively avoid household chores, why should it be a central component of a curriculum for these young people?

Special school–college link courses

3.36   Another form of separate special course is the part-time provision made within mainstream FE colleges for students in their last year at special school. The Warnock Report (DES, 1978) suggested that linked courses between special schools and colleges of further education, in which senior pupils spent half a day to two days at college, were a way of 'introducing pupils to the possibilities of further education and of widening their horizons' (para. 10.20). This social experience is one schools have increasingly sought, and link courses with colleges proliferated during the 1980s (Stowell, 1987).

3.37   In a link course, pupils in special schools get a taste of what life is like in a mainstream college of further education. I emphasize the word 'taste' for they can only get a flavour of the atmosphere, scale and scope. Most link courses are segregated. The TV programme *Linking into the Future*, which you will watch later in this section as part of your study of policy and practice in the London borough of Haringey, illustrates the advantages and disadvantages of a link course, from the students' point of view.

3.38   In 1988 I asked special schools in fifteen different LEAs about their perceptions of how link courses were influencing the programme for their senior pupils and I found some examples of schools which could offer quite extensive curricular choice in a wide range of colleges

(Corbett, 1989b). However, many schools indicated that their link courses were not really serving their needs. They often focused upon 'social and life skills' like cooking, shopping, cleaning and budgeting, as well as role play and discussion related to personal relationships. Generally, special schools felt that they could do these things better themselves. In a follow-up research project (Corbett, 1990b), teachers from schools in the original group told me how the college link courses contributed to their curriculum for senior pupils and in what ways they could be improved. Many of these teachers were challenging the traditional link which, like the course you will see later in the television programme, was segregated and focused upon social rather than academic progression. They felt that parents, pupils and teachers in the schools had raised their expectations of post-school provision and were seeking courses which could offer the following: accreditation, so that the completion of link courses was validated by a recognized qualification; a choice of modules, or short courses of study, in which students were integrated with mainstream senior pupils also on links; more two-way collaboration between school and college, so that components offered on the link contributed directly to the school curriculum; real-life problem-solving approaches adopted by both school and college, to ease students away from the individualized learning programmes which were often a feature of their early school experiences.

Funding links

3.39   Funds from the Technical and Vocational Educational Initiative (TVEI) had been used by these schools to improve the quality and smooth operation of their link. Some headteachers were using TVEI to alter the 14–16 curriculum overall, moving their staff from a subject-based curriculum to a more modular approach. (For more discussion of the TVEI scheme and how resources made available have influenced curriculum development for teenagers in schools, see Section 4.)

3.40   Not all schools used TVEI money to extend link courses. Some chose to offer a wider range of direct work-experience opportunities instead, including work on farms, riding stables and in horticulture. Where special schools belonged to a regional consortium, their joint funding strength enabled them to gain access to several college departments in different colleges, extending curricular opportunities for their pupils. Some schools used TVEI funding to buy in support staff which enabled individual pupils to select from a range of modules, rather than have to move with the group. Other schools used TVEI money to buy in tailor-made courses designed specifically for their student group. The main benefit of the TVEI funding was that it put a stop to the previously dependent status of special schools in relation to the FE colleges, who accepted their students as an act of charity.

Contrasts between school and college – attending a link course

Dawn, a student attending a link course at Haringey College, 1990 (see TV6).

Equipment in the nursery class playground at the Vale special school.

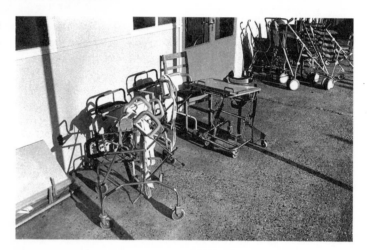

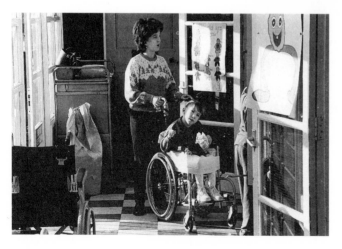

At the Vale school

A corridor in the Vale school.

(Below) Canteen, Harringey College.

(Below) Recreation in the lunch-hour, Harringey, College.

3.41   One headteacher indicates the extent of the change:

> We are going to make quite sure, in quite an uncompromising way, that we have a clear idea of what our curriculum is and to ensure that it is broad and balanced when it is linked into the college one. I think the funding arrangements have made a big difference because before you really did just have to scratch backs and do whatever you could – completely unsatisfactory and not at all right. One wasn't in a position to say, 'I'm not happy about the curriculum' because we weren't in a remotely bargaining position, whereas we're now on an equal footing in theory.
>
> (Headteacher of special school, quoted in Corbett, 1990b, p. 16)

Links for the 1990s

3.42   Demographic change has meant a greatly reduced number of young people coming through into further education in the early 1990s. This has led to college staff becoming more responsive than before:

> They are much more prepared to say, 'What do you want? We can run certain things. Is there anything else you would like us to do?' They are very much in the market place now.
>
> (Teacher, quoted in Corbett, 1990b, p. 17)

Part of this 'market-place' mentality includes a focus on 'enterprise' and 'entitlement' which, together with the demands of the National Curriculum, is altering the relationship between special schools and colleges of further education.

3.43   Many teachers said their students were entitled to participate in the same vocational curriculum offered to other students entering further education. Link courses which offered social integration but no opportunities for progression to accredited courses were being challenged:

> If you get functional integration right, the social integration will follow. The traditional link philosophy was to get your special school students out and mix them up socially with mainstream in the coffee bars and in the refectories, but I feel that we've got to give them the same sort of options that we give all our youngsters. There are lots of people I integrate with on a professional basis, on a functional basis, but I don't want to meet with out of school. Equally, there are some people I integrate on two levels with. Functional integration should be our goal.
>
> (Headteacher of special school, quoted in Corbett, 1990b, p. 16)

The implications here are that social integration entails a degree of artificiality and rests on the assumption that putting people together creates social interchange.

3.44   In discussing link courses between special schools and FE colleges, I have highlighted three main factors that have contributed to their substantial revision: first, the traditional segregated link course is no longer acceptable to many teachers; secondly, the funding provided through TVEI has extended both the range and the quality of provision; thirdly, the demands of the National Curriculum for 'breadth' and 'balance' has caused special schools to use link schemes to supplement what they themselves can provide.

MOVING TOWARDS INTEGRATED FE

3.45 There is pressure on mainstream FE colleges to respond to the following challenges:

(a) Segregated link courses need to be replaced by a range of optional modular courses for all fourteen- to sixteen-year-olds.

(b) The ethos of 'curricular entitlement' indicates that further groups of students have to be accommodated within the FE colleges: those who have severe physical or sensory disabilities and those whose behaviour is regarded as uncomfortably challenging.

(c) Links should extend into the community beyond school to reach people in day centres, who are entitled to continuing educational opportunities within further education.

3.46 However, these challenges have to be set within an increasingly competitive 'enterprise education', in which groups who are unable to invest marketable skills may become increasingly marginalized. The challenge within the transition from school to college is to recognize that parental pressures and new attitudes to integration will make this a more open and flexible stage.

Activity 4 From mainstream school to college

Read 'Abigail defies the odds' (overleaf). Recently, there have been several initiatives nationally which have led to children with Down's syndrome attending mainstream primary schools. Some of these children have gone through into secondary school. Abigail is an example.

• What do you think has been the major benefit to her of this mainstream experience?

• How far does it make you challenge the notion of special school–college link courses?

3.47 Abigail's own expectations have been influenced by her experience. From what we read in the article, she has gained an understanding of her capabilities and has both realistic expectations and an eagerness to try out new tasks. It is unlikely that she would have been aiming for an

Oxfordshire Down's syndrome girl to take two GCSEs

Abigail defies the odds

Abigail Luckett, who will sit GCSEs in rural science and childcare this term, may be the first child in the country with Down's syndrome to take the exams at the same time as the rest of her year group. Other children with Down's syndrome have taken GCSEs, but they have been older than 16-year-old Abigail.

For her parents, Abigail's achievements are a vindication of their struggle to make sure that she went to mainstream schools. Although it is now more common to integrate Down's children into ordinary schools, the Down's Syndrome Association believes that very few children of Abigail's age have spent all their time in mainstream schools.

"We have had to make sacrifices to keep Abigail in the mainstream, but I would advise any parent that if their child can cope, they should insist," said her mother, Elaine Luckett.

The family moved to Oxfordshire when Abigail was nine because the county has units for children with special needs attached to mainstream schools.

"We were very keen she should stay with normal children so we looked towards Oxfordshire. It meant a long

by Geraldine Hackett

journey to work for her father," said Mrs Luckett.

The fight started when Abigail was five and the family lived on the Isle of Wight. The local primary school finally agreed to have Abigail three days a week on a six-week trial. She stayed there for two years. "Abigail could read when she was five. I am a qualified teacher and I taught her at home for two days in the week," said Mrs Luckett.

When the family moved to Hertfordshire – her father was appointed head of a middle school in the county – Abigail went to the local church primary. She coped in a class of 30 with no extra help.

"After her second year there it was decided, after talks with the educational psychologist, that she needed more specialist help," said Mrs Luckett. It was then the family moved to Thame in Oxfordshire and Abigail attended the unit attached to John Hampden primary school.

At 11, Abigail transferred to Lord Williams's comprehensive school, which also has a special unit. She has been spending 60 per cent of her time in the unit and the rest with her tutor group.

As well as her two GCSEs, she has been following GCSE courses in drama and keyboarding, though she will not be taking them to exam level.

"She is not a worrier and she knows she can only do her best," said her mother. "She has achieved more than we ever imagined was possible."

In the future, Abigail would like to work with animals. This autumn she will go to Aylesbury College of Further Education in Buckinghamshire to do an agricultural course.

(Source: Times Educational Supplement, 18 May 1990, p. A5)

agricultural course had she remained in a special school. It is much more probable that she would have gone automatically into the college link course.

3.48 Does the transfer from special school to special college course perpetuate low expectations? Are 'social and life skills' more important than following a specific vocational area? What options might be open to Abigail in the future? Probably not a segregated day centre. Experiencing mainstream schooling has implications for further education and beyond. The effect on extending possibilities is undeniable.

3.49 Much has been written about the need for student 'empowerment' (e.g. Fenton and Hughes, 1989; Firth and Rapley, 1990; Sutcliffe, 1990). The term refers to people with disabilities or learning difficulties taking responsibility for their own lives, making decisions and directing others to carry out tasks that they are unable to do for themselves. How can this work in practice?

Activity 5 Setting the agenda for empowerment

In 'Setting the agenda: student participation on a multi-media learning scheme' (Reader 1, Chapter 6), Stuart Olesker describes a course that began in 1982 and is, essentially, a specialized course for a separated population of students. However, these students devise their own projects. They are encouraged to develop collaboration across courses with students working at a range of academic levels and they participate in a self-assessment strategy by preparing their own 'portrait portfolios'.

Read the chapter, making some notes in answer to the following questions:

- What does 'empowerment' mean in the context of the students on the Portsmouth multi-media learning scheme?

- In what ways do the form and the content of the multi-media scheme vary from what you know of FE college courses? What are its most important features?

- In what ways are students integrated into college life?

- In what ways other than strictly educational do the students on the scheme stand to benefit?

- Are there any disadvantages for students on the scheme?

- How has Stuart Olesker, a lecturer, attempted to bring alive the experience of his students in the way he has written his chapter?

3.50 Empowerment is not just about exercising choice, as it has sometimes been portrayed, but is also about active participation, such as during the multi-media scheme meeting. It is demanding and difficult. It will not accommodate pre-planned teaching objectives and curriculum frameworks. As the chapter shows, a wide range of educational, political and social issues are raised by students as urgent concerns, including 'next term's curriculum'. The students can work with staff to define and prioritize their own needs. The approach is radical in the sense that students have come into the scheme knowing what they do not want, having already rejected the conventional pattern proposed for them.

3.51 Stuart Olesker and his colleagues encourage 'error-permitted learning'. So many courses for these students have clearly set teaching objectives which they either achieve or fail. If it is anticipated that they will fail, they might not be allowed to take the risk. Individualized programmes may be negotiated by staff and students, but students are guided within an initial assessment of their skills. 'Error-permitted learning' implies that it is the learning process itself which is of value and that making errors is a valuable part of that process.

3.52 Through joint work with students working towards a range of qualifications, the multi-media students are encouraged to value their own ideas and to engage collaboratively in practical designs which will meet their immediate and long-term needs. As an exercise in empowerment it could not be more relevant. They are valued in high-quality and imaginative tasks which they would not be able to do alone. The projects are useful and, through this process, the personal becomes political.

3.53 Students like Jane take responsibility for others who may have more severe disabilities and, through a shared experience, help to make all their lives more interesting and sociable. The use of the 'portrait portfolios' enables many diverse aspects of the students' lives to be part of their learning experience. The notion of success or failure in achieving specific tasks is irrelevant and that narrow definition of learning meaningless. The promotion of 'appropriate behaviours', which is an integral part of many special college courses training students to develop social skills, is here challenged. We see the student group behaving with maturity and tolerance over what, in another context, might be seen as an unacceptable tantrum from one of their fellow-students.

3.54 As Stuart Olesker says, this scheme, which is open, accessible and encourages 'celebration of differences', is dangerous in that 'this will attract problems of security, focus and organisation' (p. 82). Yet the element of risk inherent in allowing student empowerment is surely compensated for by the unexpected emergence of talents which such an approach permits. It is the unpredictability of the scheme which allows it to be an 'educational' experience for the students, rather than a 'training' experience.

3.55 Apart from the educational benefits of the scheme, Stuart Olesker notes that students are supported to overcome depression and to make constructive use of their anger. They are enabled to raise their expectations of their own capabilities. He presents his discussion as if through the eyes of a potential student, 'Michael' – not quite a first-person account and not quite a third-person account. Did you find the style effective? Would it have been better if the students' own voices could have been heard more loudly?

3.56   Olesker's experiences are not yet typical and many FE colleges retain a skills-based, more tightly structured programme for their special courses, which are rarely integrated in the manner he describes. Patterns of course provision vary according to college policy and historical accident.

Courses for an equitable life

3.57   Not only do students transfer from special schools to colleges of further education; their teachers do as well. Maureen Turnham made the transition from teacher to lecturer in 1984 and she has written about the changes that she, her students and the college have undergone since then.

Activity 6   Supporting students in an FE college

Now read 'Supporting special needs in further education' by Maureen Turnham, which is Reader 2, Chapter 12.

As you read, make some notes in answer to the following questions:

- What was Maureen Turnham originally employed by the college to do? How and why did her view of her job evolve and change?

- How did she set about reforming the curricula available to the students with learning difficulties and what obstacles did she face? How far was she able to overcome them?

3.58   Many staff in further education who were employed specifically to work with students with learning difficulties were, like Maureen Turnham, recruited from the special school sector. This had the advantage that they were experienced in providing support learning but had the significant disadvantage that they knew nothing about the way in which further education operates. As Turnham recognizes, her naivety about the world of further education prevented her being able to adapt quickly. *She* had to be integrated first before she integrated the students she was supporting. As can be seen from her reflections, provision in colleges for disabled students has been *ad hoc* and often dismal, with the most makeshift and unsatisfactory conditions considered 'good enough' for this group.

3.59   The curriculum had developed over a period of time in which student numbers grew as careers officers were directing students towards the college. Where there is limited choice, this increase may be a reflection of taking the only provision available rather than of selecting the best or most appropriate. As Turnham indicates, she saw it as a healthy move when students began to cut the classes they found boring – in other words, to behave like 'normal' students. Her tale of the white ankle socks illustrates the problem in trying to define 'appropriate behaviour' for independent adults!

3.60   In order to have any lasting impact on the system, Turnham had to build bridges with management. Professional relationships were complex and intensely competitive, with inter-departmental rivalry requiring skilled political negotiation and calculated dealing for resources. It is no wonder that staff who came in to support students who had a low status in the college were usually at the lowest lecturer grades and operating either solo or with very small teams of colleagues, in no position to become politically powerful; who is 'on your side' then becomes vitally important. As with the social workers in Islington in the mid 1980s whom you read about in Unit 5, if there is no top-down support for change, achieving an agreed or lasting policy may be impossible.

3.61   The demands of the 'market-place' within further education militate against providing adequate support for groups of students whose academic progress and economic prospects are unlikely to bring profit to the institution. Fighting for staffing, resources and opportunities for progression for these students can hardly be left to their support staff alone. What Turnham terms 'patchwork planning' is no longer adequate and her call is for 'a blueprint for services that have commitment, consultation and collaboration ingrained'. The now popular notion of 'entitlement' has to be seen as a civil right, backed by government legislation.

3.62   Turnham insisted on calling her group 'life preparation' students. But this still begs the question, 'What sort of life?' While all other students in further education are following specific courses related to subject areas like mathematics or French or to vocational areas like carpentry, these students are preparing for life itself. I suggest that this emphasizes their marginalized status in society and implies that they are not eligible for real life, as if being trained in the annexe prepares them for the 'annexe of life'.

3.63   However, what Turnham valuably records is that important changes were happening from 1984, when she started, until the time of writing in 1991. Parent power was a force making colleges offer a viable alternative to the training centres. Self-advocacy has led to a changed attitude towards students with learning difficulties. If they want to behave 'inappropriately', then why not? What is 'appropriate' behaviour for sixteen- to nineteen-year-olds anyway?

3.64   Turnham shows that disabled students are oppressed, both with the kindness that awards them a childlike status and by the deep-rooted and simultaneous hostility that rejects them as full members of the college community.

3.65   Turnham reflects on her own acquiescence in a selection procedure that picked out for admission those students most likely to be acceptable in terms of their abilities and interests. She acknowledges that this was inequitable and contrary to her commitment to a policy of equal opportunities and to the countering of the fear, ignorance and prejudice that the students experienced in the college. She was aware that, if her colleagues came to accept her, then they were more likely to accept those they still saw as 'her' students.

3.66   This chapter has a particular meaning for me as it recalls my own experiences in a similar post. I, too, transferred from the special school sector to further education and experienced a considerable culture shock. When some of my students were integrated on a course for which they were ill-qualified, some of the mainstream students objected and complained that their exam results would be adversely affected. The students with disabilities and learning difficulties were placed in a 'caring' section of the college, with predominantly women tutors and female students who were training as nursery nurses or hairdressers. What does this say about attitudes to disability? Is disability a feminist issue? Should it become the preserve of 'caring women' only? The issues Turnham raises are political. She and I both trod through the minefield with caution and cunning. From our lowly positions in the hierarchy, we could do nothing else.

Equal opportunities and integration at Kingsway College

3.67   One FE college which has established that provision for disabled students has to be seen as part of an equal opportunities policy is Kingsway College in Camden, London. Describing the integration of these students at Kingsway, Carolyn O'Grady shows how the management structure reflects this commitment:

> Vice principal, Sue Sandle, has responsibility for equal opportunities. Reporting to her are a multi-ethnic education co-ordinator and the co-ordinator for disability who chairs the standing committee for special needs, a sub-committee of the academic board, and also sits on the course monitoring committee representing students with special needs.

> The co-ordinator for disability – Liz Maudslay – is also a member of the co-ordinating group which considers how equal opportunities can be integrated into the curriculum.

> (O'Grady, 1990, pp. 18–19)

3.68   However, Kingsway College has experienced many difficulties which are a legacy of its history and of the compromise of restricted resources. Integration has been evolving there for twenty years but has not escaped the establishment of specialist link and full-time courses, taught by 'subject specialists and learning difficulty specialists working as a team' (p. 18). Whatever policy of equal opportunities is proposed, if specialist staff are *in situ* they are often perceived as those with responsibility for students with disabilities and learning difficulties. As Liz Maudslay says:

> We're trying to get away from the situation where teachers come up to me and talk about 'one of your students' or think they are not involved because they don't have people with disabilities in their classes.

> (Maudslay, quoted in O'Grady, 1990, p. 21)

3.69   Other persistent difficulties include the following:

- the vital role of assistants who command low pay and status;

- the constant dilemmas over physical access, always excluding certain areas of the college and making daily life awkward for students or staff in wheelchairs;

- reliance on special buses and taxis which can leave students with disabilities waiting for long periods and feeling separate from their peers.

All these difficulties were familiar to me when working in further education in the mid 1980s and they remain familiar to Liz Maudslay in 1990.

Promoting positive images

3.70   An important feature of an equal opportunities policy must be a concerted attack on negative and rejecting attitudes, which has the active support and backing of senior managers. Here is what Carolyn O'Grady wrote about the promotion of positive images of disability at Kingsway:

> As part of a general equal opportunities policy a lot of effort goes into encouraging positive images of disability among pupils and staff. 'Getting positive images of disability into the curriculum of able-bodied students is as important as supporting the disabled students', says Sue Sandle.
>
> Ways are constantly sought to encourage students to think about disability in a positive and practical way. BTEC science students, for example, have worked on a project to adapt a laboratory for scientists who are disabled.
>
> #### Subtle prejudice
>
> The reaction of students to integration appears to be positive. According to Liz Maudslay, there are probably fewer anti-disability instances than cases of racism or sexism, although she points out that prejudice against disabled people may be expressed in subtle ways, for instance, through being patronising.
>
> The mature blind student finds the attitude of other students 'brilliant – very different from the people in the street, who just think you are thick. One student has totally adopted me and waits for me in a very natural, matter-of-fact way.'
>
> (O'Grady, 1990, p. 20)

3.71   As we saw in Stuart Olesker's chapter, when staff encourage students to work together to design aids and improve access, this helps to produce positive attitudes. In the project for BTEC science students at Kingsway, the daily needs of people with specific disabilities are addressed. This has improved understanding while, at the same time, improving facilities.

Staff development

> Supporting staff is a primary task for effective integration in Sue Sandle's opinion. Many teachers suffer from lack of confidence on top of the other constraints of lack of money, resources and time. 'Some staff will have stereotyped ideas and the lack of confidence springs from this. When we talk about actual people, the stereotypes break down. When staff members are faced with students with disabilities they have to get down to the nitty gritty and they do.'
>
> (O'Grady, 1990, pp. 20–21)

3.72   As Sue Sandle says, staff need support at a practical, personal level. Policy documents alone will not suffice. Recognizing fears and anxieties is important. The change in attitudes is supported by a delicate balance which combines an obligation to share responsibility with an acknowledgement of the ensuing demands.

3.73   Such staff training initiatives have to come from management. One of the difficulties experienced by many special needs co-ordinators in colleges is that they are expected to engage in staff development while commanding low status in the college hierarchy. Colleges of further education are often patriarchal establishments, in which male staff will only respond seriously to those in positions of authority. It is because Sue Sandle is a vice principal that she is able to effect a change in staff attitudes through supporting disability awareness.

3.74   Staff training packs like *Learning Support* (Faraday and Harris, 1989) can also provide valuable practical guidelines. This pack, for example, includes advice on modifying aspects of a mainstream course to accommodate a wider range of learners. In relation to managing the setting, staff are encouraged to place 'slower learners, with faster learners' which 'allows some mutual support and exchange to take place, enhancing the learning for all participants' (p. 15). The guidance is essentially geared to daily practice, including suggested room arrangements, teaching methods and use of varied resources.

FURTHER EDUCATION IN HARINGEY

3.75   This sub-section focuses on developments in further education in the north London borough of Haringey. A brief description of the borough is followed by an account of the opening of Haringey College in 1983 and the policy of equality of opportunity to which it was committed from the start. The television programme *Linking into the Future* takes a close look at how this policy has worked out in practice for some of the students at Haringey College. Discussion of this programme forms the core of this section.

3.76   The population of Haringey includes a large proportion of people of Caribbean, Greek or Turkish Cypriot, Asian, and African origins. In the poorest areas of the borough, such as Tottenham, the percentage of residents of Caribbean origin is higher. In its recent history, the borough has been regarded as a problem area. Haringey was classed with three other LEAs (out of a total of 97) as having the highest level of pupils likely to experience difficulties in school as a result of poverty and deprivation (DES, 1982). An HMI report of 1984 recorded higher rates of unemployment than in Greater London as a whole, with the highest rates among the young. Exam achievements were lower than average: the percentage of fifth-year pupils gaining no graded result was 18 per cent as against 10 per cent nationally (DES, 1984). The HMI report suggested low expectations generally and a lack of cohesion in in-service support in schools. Teacher shortages have been particularly acute in areas like Tottenham, which endures all the stigma associated with tense inner-city areas. Some parents have been so dissatisfied with the low demands being made of their children within the state sector that they have established an independent all-black school within Tottenham (Baker, 1985). The Broadwater Farm riots of 1985 contributed further to the image of an area which was potentially dangerous and hostile.

3.77   In December 1989, Chris Shellard, Haringey's education officer for post-16 provision, said:

> I would estimate in Haringey that somewhere in the region of 25 per cent of the population could fall into a 'special needs' category. That is very much a local estimate and it may be that it is higher than that. We've decided to give twice the unit of resource to special needs students than to ordinary students who may be following a general education programme.
>
> (Shellard, interviewed for E877, Open University, 1990)

3.78   Chris Shellard's estimate indicates that Haringey's population, especially in areas like Tottenham, hardly reflects Warnock's elusive 18 per cent (DES, 1978) but rather the effects of high socio-economic deprivation:

> Historically, equality of opportunity has not and does not exist for large numbers of the populace, who both within and after school experience the personal, social and economic effects of failure.
>
> (Barton and Tomlinson, 1984, p. 79)

3.79   In the most deprived areas of Haringey there are communities which have produced a high proportion of children who are seen as having 'moderate learning difficulties' or 'emotional and behavioural difficulties'. The proportion of black pupils in Haringey's special school for children with emotional and behavioural difficulties in the mid 1980s reflected Tomlinson's (1981) findings that a disproportionate number of children from minority ethnic groups were placed in such provision.

3.80 Tottenham College of Technology, a long-established regional provision offering a wide range of vocational and academic courses, appeared to be in an ideal location to service its more immediate local community as well, situated as it is on Tottenham High Road. However, its regional status meant that it provided only a limited number of courses for local residents. A second FE college, Haringey College, was therefore established in 1983 to meet these local needs.

Haringey College

3.81 The principal, Ethelyne Prince, one of the few black women in such a post, described the policy which underlay practice at the college:

> This college was established in 1983 primarily to meet the needs of the local community. Against that background, given that the authority was essentially concerned with ensuring that students who may well be considered as 'second-chancers' may not have reached their full potential, that every opportunity should be provided within this college for them to do so. It is in that context that one should understand the student profile of this college.
>
> (Prince, interviewed in 1989 for TV6 *Linking into the Future*)

3.82 It was part of the policy of Haringey College deliberately to encourage those students into post-sixteen provision who had in the past not usually continued with their education beyond school. This meant that the 'student profile' the principal refers to involved a high proportion of students identified as having some kind of 'special educational need' exacerbated by social disadvantage. Waveney Harries, head of the special needs department at Haringey College, estimated that this group amounted to one in eight of the student population of the college.

A whole-college policy on equal opportunities

3.83 This attitude to student admission was reflective of the equal opportunities policy which was central to the college ethos and which covered especially issues related to sexism, racism and disability. As the principal stated:

> In the case of special needs, that there should be no discrimination based on their disabilities. Equally, when one looks at other members of the student body, that there should be no discrimination on the grounds of colour, race, sex, nationality, religion or things of this nature.
>
> (Interview, 1989)

3.84 All staff and students at Haringey College were made aware of this policy when they started at the college; the climate was such that any examples of discriminatory practice were treated seriously as a breach of the college policy.

Staff development and disability awareness

3.85   Putting a policy of equal opportunities into practice can require careful planning. Staff development, supported by management, may be necessary to dissolve any initial resistance. For example, during enrolment, specialist staff can work alongside mainstream staff to identify student requirements. In this collaborative approach, students, mainstream and specialist staff inform one another and some possible misunderstandings can be avoided.

3.86   Harries recognized that 'inevitably, there are negative attitudes and it is something that has to be worked at and confronted'. This can include influencing the attitudes of mainstream students:

> Staff from the unit went into tutorial sessions throughout the college to talk to mainstream students about the ethos of the college and the students with special needs who were in the college. We had meetings with the admin. and reception staff. We were very keen that the students had a high profile within the institution, that their base room wasn't going to be put outside the college. It was going to be in the main college corridor. They were going to be seen in every possible circumstance ... it was very important for us that they were involved in all the college activities that they could join in.
>
> (Harries, 1990, p. 43)

3.87   Attention to attitudes and awareness extended through all aspects of college life, including lunch-times and recreation:

> Trying to alter entrenched attitudes proved to be a difficult task. Canteen staff 'felt sorry' for the students and extra portions of chips, as well as free helpings on demand [were] a common occurrence at first.
>
> A visual menu was provided by the teaching staff and copies were put up near the serving hatches and around the college generally. Students were encouraged to queue appropriately and go through the system of collecting their trays and utensils.
>
> ... Other areas of integration were then approached. The college has an Open Recreation session every Wednesday afternoon and it was felt that this would be an ideal next step. We introduced only a small number of students at a time and again staff of the Special Needs Unit worked beside staff of the Leisure and Recreation department. Mainstream students were asked to make up foursomes for badminton and table-tennis where appropriate.
>
> The sports hall was very much a male macho stronghold and students who were into the 'body beautiful' had their image ruined with the arrival of the students with special needs! After a few incidents, where students refused to stay in the hall when the students arrived, one of the particularly talented students with autism designed the most dramatic poster announcing that 'This

Gym is for Everyone to Enjoy' – it worked and Wednesday afternoon recreation is now an established part of the curriculum.

(Harries, 1990, pp. 43–4)

Curriculum and teaching approaches

3.88   I have described how a separate special curriculum became established in mainstream further education for particular groups of students. This is still common, particularly for students with severe learning difficulties. However, policies within colleges are gradually changing so that a range of pre-vocational courses are offered, catering for students with a wider diversity of abilities. One of the most popular courses of this type is the Certificate of Pre-Vocational Education (CPVE) which permits students to try different options, like building, hairdressing, typing, catering, community care or computing and which can lead on to other vocational courses. For example, CPVE community care can lead to a nursery nursing course. The course structure is not dissimilar in format from Youth Training (YT) options, but it operates solely on college premises and students do not qualify for a training allowance. (See Section 4 for a further discussion of CPVE.)

3.89   Do practical subjects lend themselves more easily to integrated practice? Terry Kill, tutor on the CPVE health and community care course at Haringey College, found it most effective to:

> treat the students with 'special needs' much as any other student. I suppose that would be our starting point. We try to do nothing different, but some of the students have specific problems, for example, physical disabilities. If you were asking Paula to cut with scissors she finds it very difficult so we would do that for her. Other students might have specific learning difficulties so we would have to consider any numeracy or communication demands that we might make on them.

> (Kill, interviewed in 1989 for TV6)

3.90   Far from the inclusion of some students proving disadvantageous to others, Kill felt that the range of abilities and interests represented in the group brought positive benefits for all the students:

> We have a module on 'The Care of Those with Disabilities' and obviously if within that option you've got students with disabilities it changes the whole tenor of the discussion. Generally speaking, I think it makes people realize that we are all human beings and we are all different and some disabilities are more visible than others.

> (Interview, 1989)

Activity 7   Linking into the future

Now watch TV6, *Linking into the Future: a college community,* which was filmed in 1989 in Haringey College.

You will see three main groups of students in the programme:

(a) students from the Vale special school who are attending Haringey College on a part-time specialist link course (see pp. 24–5);

(b) students on a full-time integrated CPVE health and community care course;

(c) students on a full-time separate 'learning for life' course.

We begin with student Dawn, whom we see first at home and at school.

We later see the link course students in the multi-skills workshop, working alongside a group of day-release students following a City and Guilds craft course.

On the CPVE course, Karen and Paula work together and have become friends as a result.

Students on the 'learning for life' course are going off to the local library, rehearsing for an independence that may turn out to be elusive when they leave college (opposite).

As you watch the programme, make some notes in answer to the following questions:

• What seem to you to be the advantages and disadvantages of enrolling on a link course?

• What seem to be the possibilities of and limits to full participation within the mainstream of Haringey College for all students?

• How far does 'social integration' develop if students do not actually work together?

3.91   Dawn says in the film:

> They treat you more like adults. You can make your own way around and that is really good. I was nervous when I first went, then I gradually worked myself in. There are too many stairs and slopes and I need help with opening and closing doors.

The link course gives Dawn a chance to 'work herself in' before she starts her full-time course the following year. That course, the CPVE, will be integrated.

Travel training

Preparation: discussion in class.

Crossing the road to go to the bus stop.

Discussion with the teacher on the way to the library.

Choosing a book in the library.

3.92   When we see the link course group working in the multi-skills workshop, the lecturer who is teaching them tells us that they are a 'mixed group', who have come from different special schools. They include pupils variously labelled as having 'moderate learning difficulties', 'severe learning difficulties' and 'emotional and behavioural difficulties'. Does it seem strange to you that pupils selected for a specialist education, on the grounds of specific individual need, should then be 'mixed' with other 'special' groups? This would not appear to be to their advantage, creating potential frustrations for staff trying to offer a range of collaborative learning experiences.

3.93   When asked about social integration, one of the City and Guilds course students says, 'They do their thing. We do ours.' Yet the lecturer taking the link course group says that the whole value of the link is *not* the subject matter but the fact that they are integrating with other students. Who is right? Are they just working alongside with no interaction or are they being mutually enriched by the experience?

3.94   On the CPVE course, Karen reflects on her early awareness of Paula's disability:

> When I first went in the class you wouldn't know that Paula was disabled when she was sitting down. When she got up and walked it was a real shock but I'd already started talking to her so it didn't make no difference really.

Paula and Karen were working collaboratively on an integrated course. They started out on the course as equals, and, despite her shock, Karen could not perceive Paula as different. This contrasts with the workshop sequence, where the two groups are very aware of their difference and neither side appears to seek social interaction.

3.95   The benefits of 'social integration' seem to be elusive. Groups who perceive themselves as different will rarely mix socially. They tend to stay together as a group in the canteen and the common room. Neither 'locational' or 'social' integration (using the terminology of the Warnock Report) seem to be appropriate as part of any real attempt to create an integrated community.

3.96   Since the television programme was made, opportunities for the students have altered drastically. First, the college itself has merged with Tottenham College to form the North East London College. A white man was appointed principal and the former black woman principal of Haringey College has become a vice principal of the combined college. Severe and extensive poll-tax-capping in the borough has resulted in a reduction of support and less satisfactory provision for the students. Staff who have developed effective integration as part of equal opportunities have seen this eroded as different priorities take precedence. These changes represent the panic measures to which a local government is reduced to taking when financial crisis determines policy. National changes are also altering methods of assessment, and a system of National Vocational Qualifications (NVQs) is threatening the continuation of CPVE courses.

Higher education

(a) Very few students with disabilities or learning difficulties progress into higher education. Special schooling limits opportunities to obtain the required level of qualifications. Physical access is often a barrier for students who use wheelchairs who may therefore have to select from a limited range of options.

(b) Equal opportunities policies in higher education have led to the establishment of 'named persons' to support students with disabilities or learning difficulties, although this is not included within national policy.

(c) Changes in course structure and teaching approaches in higher education are likely to make many areas of the curriculum more accessible. Flexibility and a student-centred focus can be seen not only to make higher education more integrated but also to fulfil government plans for future expansion.

Further education

(a) Further education is a sector which is experiencing considerable changes. These changes will influence provision for students with disabilities and learning difficulties, which has become an integral, if peripheral, part of further education. Integration in further education has developed over the 1980s from being a selective and charitable model, unsupported by resources, to being a part of equal opportunities policy within a whole-college approach.

(b) The special FE colleges tend to offer provision for students with complex difficulties. They have often adopted a 'life-skills' curriculum which is designed to prepare young people with disabilities or learning difficulties for life in the community.

(c) The link courses operating between special schools and colleges are changing. The influence of TVEI and the National Curriculum has made relevance, breadth of curriculum and opportunities for progression key aims. The very need for such special provision is being challenged within a new focus upon curriculum entitlement.

(d) Staff with responsibility for students placed in 'special needs' sections of FE colleges have generally been given low status. As responsibility for *all* students, regardless of gender, race or disability, is becoming a whole-college commitment, so the status of special needs co-ordinators is changing. More are now in managerial posts, with a degree of control over staffing and resources. Successful staff training throughout a college is dependent upon the level of active involvement shown by senior members of the college hierarchy.

(e) Current government legislation is prioritizing outcomes and income-generation which jeopardizes provision for students with learning difficulties. The broadly educative function of further education is threatened by an emphasis on training for employment. Voluntary bodies like Skill act as vociferous advocates on behalf of students with disabilities and learning difficulties, ensuring that their needs are included on the political agenda.

(f) The United Kingdom lags behind other European countries in its school 'staying-on' rate and in the numbers of students proceeding into further and higher education. Sixteen-year-olds are still leaving compulsory schooling with a feeling that they are academic failures and that they really want a job. The government White Paper on further education and training for the twenty-first century (DES, 1991) is an attempt to address this issue.

4 FROM SCHOOL TO WORK, OR NOT

4.1   In this section, the transition from school to an adult life is discussed in relation to employment, unemployment and pre-employment vocational training. Social status in UK society is crucially influenced by the nature of the paid work people do. Unemployment carries a social stigma, and the inability to earn a regular wage may deprive a person of adult status altogether. Yet for some people, those who have a severe physical disability for example, the fullest extent of their social participation may be a life without work within, rather than outside, their community and neighbourhood.

TRAINING AND EMPLOYMENT

4.2   The job market for all young people has shrunk dramatically. The kind of work available has also changed. For example, Griffiths (1989) outlines employment opportunities for young people leaving school without formal qualifications:

> A simple figure of jobs available can mask changes which have taken place in the type of jobs on offer. For example a laundry which provided 50 jobs may close and instead two estate agents, three specialist retail outlets for electronic goods, a restaurant and a solicitor's office may open in the same area. There will have been no statistical job loss but most of the ex-laundry employees may become unemployed because they cannot be recruited for the new jobs. New arrivals or commuters from another area fill them. This has implications both for geographical areas and for certain groups of job seekers.
>
> (Griffiths, 1989, p. 12)

4.3   Here is another example: a national supermarket chain has altered its practice so that *all* members of in-store staff are expected to take turns with *all* jobs, moving from packing shelves to shifting trolleys to working the check-out till. While this has significant advantages for the majority of staff, in that it offers variety and relief from boredom, it was greatly to the disadvantage of those employees with difficulties in learning, whose job it had formerly been to pack shelves and clear trolleys. They were unable to cope with the check-out tills and, therefore, were redeployed. The implications for those people wanting to apply to work in the store in the future were that they would need skills which would, inevitably, exclude some who would have been employed under former conditions.

4.4   Pace is also a factor that can exclude people from employment. Graham attends a social education centre (SEC), which provides educational and recreational activities, but also some light industrial paid work. He was able to move into open employment from the SEC, but unfortunately it did not last:

> I'm a bit slow at learning things. When I left school I went to a Social Education Centre. I did weighing up nails, putting them in bags and stapling them over.

> The only reason I got a job was that Mr A (an instructor at the Social Education Centre) saw it in the paper and phoned up the laundry. I think that the decision that I should look at the job was shared between me and Mr A. I got the job at the laundry but I was sacked because I did not do it fast enough. I could do it properly but a normal person could do it more faster.

> (Graham, quoted in Griffiths, 1989, p. 45)

This example illustrates the dilemma for an employee like Graham, who is reliable but can be replaced by someone faster and more cost effective.

4.5   Support in the early stages of employment appears to make all the difference between people keeping a job or finding it too stressful (Sutcliffe, 1990). Adults who move out of social education centres into open employment face a period of great adjustment. Lorna Kingshott (1991) describes her feelings:

> When I go back to the centre on a Monday I feel that students and staff are strange towards me. In other words they don't want to know me, that's my feeling, but it's because I am in a working environment now away from the centre and mixing with new people out in the community like any other working person in this world today. It isn't easy moving away from the centre into a full-time job I can tell you, so if you are thinking about moving away from the centre into a full-time job then talk to your key worker ... or go through the right channels of a Pathway Employment Officer who can help you find a job in your area.

> (Kingshott, 1991, p. 5)

The Pathway Employment Service, to which Lorna Kingshott refers, is a provision established by MENCAP to place people in regular jobs, earning the going rate for the work they do.

Adapt to what's offered or hold out for what you want?

4.6 Cyrus wanted to work in an office but all that was available to him was work as a cleaner at the local holiday camp. His story raises the dilemma of whether it is preferable to adapt to the work that is offered and secure a job or to hold out for what you want, risking unemployment to prove that your aspirations are realistic.

> After leaving school, Cyrus spent three years at a training college for people with disabilities, where he learnt the rudiments of office practice. He then worked for a season at Butlins on a Sheltered Placement Scheme. This entailed cleaning duties, which Cyrus disliked, but with which he persevered for the complete season, despite his manual dexterity problem.
>
> In September 1987, when we first met at Cyrus's isolated home in rural Clwyd, Cyrus was bored and depressed, having been unemployed for twelve months. He was losing his confidence and beginning to question whether he would ever find a job, let alone achieve his desire to work in an office. Eventually, 29 meetings with 22 different people, and innumerable telephone calls later, we were successful in obtaining a post for Cyrus as a Clerical Assistant, and when asked how he felt now that he had finally achieved his ambition, Cyrus replied:

Cyrus working in an office.

'A lot happier and contented, generally wanted. I was told at the rehabilitation centre that I was unemployable. I have proved to myself and others that I am employable.'

(Williams, 1991, p. 4)

4.7 Is 'employability' as much to do with the availability of appropriate advice and support as it is to do with the characteristics of an individual in isolation? Griffiths (1989) found that most employers were seeking reliability and punctuality in their employees. Cyrus persevered in a job he disliked at Butlins, which was more than many young people would have done. To keep him in this new office job, however, the Pathway officer paid regular visits to Cyrus in his workplace over a nine-month period, during which time close liaison was kept up with Cyrus and his employers. Cyrus and his colleagues needed support in recognizing the degree of extra supervision he required. When he felt secure and well established, external support was gradually withdrawn.

THE 14 TO 16 CURRICULUM AND VOCATIONAL CHOICE

4.8 Curricula for school students aged fourteen to sixteen became increasingly vocational during the 1980s in an attempt to prepare young people for the harsh reality of a rapidly shrinking market for unqualified young people. Vocational training schemes for sixteen- to nineteen-year-olds also proliferated, to the extent that a large proportion of this age-group now go on to a training scheme and relatively few go straight into employment.

4.9 A vocational approach to the education of teenagers may appear to be a sensible and overdue challenge to the dominance of a narrowly academic secondary school curriculum and a way to support the transition from school to work. However, such an approach may also function to emphasize the division between 'practical' and 'academic' school work and may later turn out to have been a wasted experience, when trainees still end up without a job and realize, perhaps, that recreational courses would have stood them in better stead.

4.10 Two developments in particular made a mark on both secondary and further education in the 1980s, the Technical and Vocational Educational Initiative (TVEI) and the Certificate of Pre-Vocational Education (CPVE). The CPVE approach was discussed and illustrated in the previous section of the unit in relation to provision at Haringey College. The development of TVEI during the 1980s made perhaps the most significant impact on secondary schools across the UK until the advent of the National Curriculum in 1988 made its future uncertain.

Trainees on workshop-based Youth Training: tasting the options

Woodwork.

Catering.

Computers.

Office skills.

TVEI

4.11 TVEI began as a pilot project in 1983, introduced by the government. It aimed to bring schools into a closer relationship with the world of work. TVEI is a vocationally-oriented approach to the curriculum, and new funding supported a range of diverse initiatives. Hickox and Moore describe TVEI as follows:

> First, it is an attempt to 're-centre' the secondary curriculum around science and technology and to shift it away from the post-Newsom base in the Humanities. Secondly, to facilitate a change in fundamental educational attitudes and values towards positive support for commerce and industry and the practical application of knowledge. This reflects the view that both traditional and progressive liberal educationalists have tended to exhibit an active disdain or outright hostility towards 'enterprise' and industry and have, on the one hand, failed to meet the needs of non-academic pupils and, on the other, failed to meet the needs of the economy by encouraging the high-fliers to seek careers elsewhere (mainly in academia). Thirdly, it attempts to represent these shifts in a pedagogy which more accurately reflects the character of 'real-world' problem solving processes.
>
> (Hickox and Moore, 1990, pp. 134–5)

4.12 Cooper (1988) suggests that TVEI is valuable for all learners, as it promotes a more coherent progression of courses within secondary schools and a stronger link between school and further education or training. Shilling (1990), on the other hand, insists that 'there are almost bound to be disjunctions between schemes which operate largely in one institutional setting, *yet seek to import the concerns of a different sector of economic/social life*' (p. 183). Further, Ainley (1990) illustrates the way in which teachers learned to use TVEI funding to achieve what they had always wanted. In one school, this involved installing computer terminals in every classroom and networking with other schools in a consortium.

TVEI and students from special schools

4.13 Special schools for pupils said to have 'moderate learning difficulties' were among the first to be included in making links with industry. Shilling (1990) records the establishment of the Schools Vocational Programme (SVP) in 1976/77. Matthews (1990) notes that when a scheme known as the School Curriculum Industry Partnership (SCIP) was set up in 1977/78, 'special schools were included in the pilot scheme and the work focused on the last two years of compulsory schooling' (p. 95). She describes the main aims of this project as being:

> to bring about change in the school curriculum in order to promote students' understanding of industry and of industrial society. In doing this SCIP hoped to enable young people, regardless of ability, gender or race, to take part in shaping the future of their society.
>
> (Matthews, 1990, p. 95)

4.14   After twelve years of growth, SCIP is now addressing National Curriculum issues and its emphasis on preparation for adult life as an entitlement for all learners, including those in special schools.

Activity 8   Preparing for work

You read earlier how Cyrus both stuck at his cleaning job and stuck out for the office job that he really wanted but for which he required regular additional support. Cyrus's 'employability' was related to three factors: first, his own determination; second, the availability of continuing support on the job; and third, the relevance of his training course.

Now read the brief account below of a school-based work-experience project and make some notes in answer to these questions:

- What kinds of skills did the students develop as a result of their involvement in the project?

- How far are skills that make young people 'employable' directly related to those fostered by vocational training?

- How far has 'employability' anything to do with being an independent adult?

The Delves School, Swanwick, Derbyshire

The project was launched in an all-age, area special school with 92 pupils who had moderate learning difficulties and came from both rural communities and old-established industrial towns. The school had been accustomed to reviewing its programme to prepare pupils for post-school experience, and had done so well before the arrival of what it described as 'the current Exocets of curriculum initiatives which daily appear over the horizon'.

The school was asked for help by a local firm in the construction of wooden 'cribs' used in fire testing of the polyurethane foam which is part of three piece suites and other domestic furniture. The project began as a small-scale lunch time activity with a few interested pupils but soon expanded when the firm paid a contribution to the school for each properly completed crib and part of the payment was shared among pupils according to their output.

One of the most positive outcomes of the project was the willingness of some pupils to discuss crib-making with members of the firm – adults with whom they were not used to talking, adults who were not 'safe' and who would (so the pupils thought) not listen patiently and make allowances for them in the same way as teachers. Another positive and most interesting aspect of the project was that it allowed a pupil-centred and pupil-controlled project to develop away from the overt control of teachers in a setting which encouraged pupils to take the initiative.

Individual pupils learnt a great deal from the experience. For instance, 15-year-old Linda, the quality controller for the cribs, had to deal with disputes over rejected cribs which were not up to the firm's standard. This led to her 'sacking' of a fellow pupil for swearing at her rather than arguing his case – a step forward in the inter-personal relationships in the group. Andrew and Ian, both 16, had a private competition between them to produce the larger number of cribs, which resulted in their taking raw materials home at the weekend to continue the work. Ian improved his previously erratic attendance and gained the confidence to find his own work experience and resulting placement on the Youth Training Scheme.

(Matthews, 1990, p. 97)

4.15   It would seem that styles of behaviour, such as reliability and compliance, contribute as much, if not more, to the employability of a young person as does the acquisition of vocational skills. The kind of behaviour that seems to be valued in the workplace includes:

- taking the initiative in managing efficiency;

- meeting the required criteria and responding to being paid by output;

- displaying appropriate behaviour to those in authority;

- developing competitive motivation;

- showing commitment;

- being reliable.

4.16   This range, which seems to add up to an enthusiastic display of subordinate behaviour, is often described as 'adult' and 'independent', as if the initiative taken by these young people is really the result of maturity and choice. However, the real world of work for many young people with learning difficulties is characterized by both tedium and effort. 'Success' means accepting the discipline and repetitiveness of a boring job:

> It meant that the expectations of students should be adjusted as suitable for 'being a small cog in a large machine and having to do what are possibly very boring jobs' (local Tory). As the senior teacher put it, 'SVP is a *vocational* course, and we aim to develop attitudes which are appropriate to working in industry. This is part of the process of growing up for young people.' For the Programme's clientele, this entailed 'developing the ability to concentrate, work consistently over long periods of time, learning to be punctual and follow instructions with care and precision' (headteacher).
>
> (Shilling, 1990, p. 66)

4.17   The tensions of many of the 14 to 16 vocational initiatives are reflected in these contradictions: on the one hand, low-achievers are encouraged to experience success in new areas; on the other hand, they are being carefully nurtured to become compliant and competent unskilled workers. Thus, criticisms arise from what is apparently overt manipulation of school/industry links to serve a market economy.

A new vocationalism for the 1990s?

4.18   Despite much initial hostility towards TVEI, there has now developed among teachers a widespread acceptance of its potential benefit (Jackson, 1990). Ironically, this comes at a time when funding for TVEI projects appears to be under threat as the government changes the educational focus. While the White Paper *Better Schools* (DES, 1985) suggested that TVEI was the prototype for future educational reform, later documentation on the National Curriculum barely mentioned it. Ainley (1990) suggests that 'since then the whole purpose of TVEI has been redefined into one of merely supporting the National Curriculum' and that 'when its funding ends in 1996 the whole scheme may be officially forgotten' (p. 25).

4.19   According to the White Paper *Education and Training for the 21st Century* (DES, 1991), the government intends to promote 'Compacts', an approach to school–work links. The Compacts programme was launched in 1988 as part of the strategy to revitalize inner cities. Fifty-one Compacts had been established by 1991, involving nearly 500 schools and almost 92,000 young people. Wheeler (1990) describes the London Compact in which he participated as an employer. One of the schools in the Compact was a special school for pupils with learning difficulties. The eleven pupils who made up the school's fifth form took part in a 26-week work experience programme where they spent a day a week with an employer. Five of these pupils entered employment as a direct result of their work experience. Here, Wheeler describes the Compact methods:

> Within the Compact partnership, two weeks' work experience is one of the four goals students need to attain to become 'Compact Graduates', the three others being 85 per cent attendance, 90 per cent punctuality and the completion of the pupil's course together with accreditation or certification in English, mathematics/numeracy. In West London, 800 pupils were placed in various work experience schemes for two weeks during the summer term. Schools found that the pupils who particularly benefited were those who showed signs of disaffection and had poor attendance records. At the end of the exercise 85 per cent of pupils had been successful in completing the project.
> (Wheeler, 1990, p. 175)

4.20   His reflections reveal both the strengths and weaknesses of the new vocationalism. The relevance of work experience is an incentive. Yet this specific route is of most apparent value to the most disaffected. In its emphasis on attendance and punctuality, it provides a means of control which further divides the academic from the vocational in 'policing' a certain section of secondary pupils.

Activity 9 Students' expectations of life after school

What do young people themselves think of provision for sixteen- to nineteen-year-olds? What is their experience of the transition from school to work or from school to unemployment or from school to training schemes?

Now read 'From school to schemes: out of education into training' by Robert Hollands, which is Reader 1, Chapter 21.

As you read, make some notes in answer to the following questions:

- How far do the young people interviewed by Robert Hollands see their secondary schooling as a relevant preparation for their adult lives?

- What role does training play in their transition to adult life and how far is it related to expectations of securing open employment?

___

4.21   Robert Hollands observes that actual choices for these working-class young people were strictly limited and their opportunities seemed few. They tended to blame themselves for low achievement. Not all of them felt ready for a college course. Hollands stresses that most of them still expected to find a job on leaving school. When this proved impossible, they settled for training. He recognizes that race, gender and disability influence choice and that some young people experience more discrimination than others. He shows that choosing to go into a training programme is not a first option but a necessity. Careers officers guide young people into Youth Training (YT; now taken over from YTS) rather than jobs.

4.22   The young people who talked to Hollands had left school with a negative self-image. They had experienced stress and failure and came to see school as irrelevant to the 'real world' of work, home and community. Work-oriented courses were seen as a deceitful and patronizing way to provide for teenagers in school, a holding on to childhood rather than a moving on to adulthood. You might like to reflect on the similarities between these young people's experiences of school and those of the Scottish girls who talked to Gwynedd Lloyd (see Unit 11/12 and Reader 1, Chapter 19).

4.23   These young people had very little freedom of choice. They would probably not benefit from staying on at school after sixteen, they were not eligible for educational grants, which do not exist for further education as they do for universities, and even a college course was unlikely because of their lack of qualifications, financial support and other social difficulties. Youth Training schemes have become virtually the only option and they are now presented by careers officers as career opportunities.

4.24   The expectations of most of the young people that they would get a job on leaving school were soon dispelled and they accepted training instead. If school-based and college- or community-based vocational courses in fact lead young people nowhere near a job on completion, then what function do they have in the lives of the trainees? Should school and college curricula be reformed to reflect a different kind of relevance, encouraging a more creative and critical approach to making the transition from school to life after school? How can young people prepare themselves for the 'real world' of the 1990s?

4.25   In 1991, I investigated several training programmes in different parts of the United Kingdom for the Further Education Unit (Corbett, 1991b). The young people I talked to expressed similar views to those who talked to Robert Hollands. Their parents criticized training courses for being slave labour, although some of them welcomed the extra income that came with the allowance of £35 a week. Some trainees felt that the skills they learned were of a very low level, whereas others felt that training was a genuine career opportunity. Nearly all of the trainees wanted to remain as close to home as possible.

4.26   The trainees I interviewed were on YT or ET (Employment Training) schemes. The latter were established from 1989 for the long-term unemployed aged over eighteen. Under the influence of the Training and Enterprise Councils (TECs), many of the ET and YT programmes which accommodated trainees with disabilities or learning difficulties were the first to be closed down in 1991. As Phillips (1991) reflects, the TECs have cut the special needs training schemes as they are the most expensive and TECs are run by business people who are more preoccupied with profitable outcomes than offering opportunities to the long-term unemployed.

4.27   Ainley (1990) asks if the TECs' provision will be evaluated in relation to helping these particular young people to achieve a Level 2 National Vocational Qualification (NVQ). While several of the training managers I interviewed welcomed the coming of NVQs in order to enable their trainees to gain a foothold on the qualifications ladder, several expressed reservations as to the level of additional support which would be required. At the Annual Skill Conference in February 1992, the representative from the Council for National Vocational Qualifications was challenged by staff in colleges about the way in which the needs of young people with learning difficulties were being overlooked. Again the need for a clearly defined and focused framework seems apparent – instead of which, while under threat of possible closure, training programmes can only struggle along in the short term.

5 INVESTIGATIONS

Views on integration

5.1 In this option you investigate the views of a small group of three or four students with disabilities or learning difficulties on their experience of integration. They may be students in further or higher education. The aim is to explore their perceptions and experiences in the light of their past in compulsory schooling. Each interview should last no more than thirty minutes. You should ask your interviewees:

(a) to describe how they came into further or higher education;

(b) to discuss their choice of course and the subject areas they are pursuing;

(c) to explain the extent to which they are integrated and what they feel they gain or lose from this;

(d) to describe any changes they would like to see in the practice of equal opportunities and anti-discrimination;

(e) to consider what move they wish to make next and why.

Policy for equal opportunities

5.2 In this option you contact the special needs co-ordinator at your local college of further education. You investigate their involvement in implementing a policy for equal opportunities which includes special educational needs. You should find out:

(a) what written policy documents exist in the college and the extent to which the special needs co-ordinator was involved in helping to draft them;

(b) how this policy has been implemented since its dissemination and the extent of management commitment in terms of resourcing and staffing;

(c) the limitations of the policy and why difficulties arise which are detrimental to students and staff with a wide range of disabilities;

(d) the extent to which policy has included curriculum development and flexible teaching approaches which can broaden access.

Broadening the mainstream and special school curriculum

5.3 Has the National Curriculum led to mainstream and special schools seeking more specific links with further education, in order to extend their subject options? In this option you investigate this question by talking to a small group of three or four teachers. They might be learning support teachers or subject teachers in comprehensive schools or teachers in all-age or secondary special schools. Comparison between teachers in mainstream and special schools would be useful. Each interview should last no more than thirty minutes. You should ask your interviewees:

(a) to give details of the kind of links (e.g. TVEI, CPVE, special link courses) which they have had with colleges of further education in the past;

(b) to describe any changes in the nature of the school/college link which have developed since the introduction of the National Curriculum;

(c) to give their views on what colleges can contribute to the curriculum of senior school pupils and on how recent changes, including the government White Paper, are broadening or narrowing choices for students.

REFERENCES

AINLEY, P. (1990) *Vocational Education and Training*, London, Cassell Books.

BAKER, N. (1985) 'A school apart', *Times Educational Supplement*, **22**(11), p. 21.

BALDWIN, S. and HATTERSLEY, J. (eds) (1991) *Mental Handicap: social science perspectives*, London, Routledge.

BARTON, L. and TOMLINSON, S. (1984) 'The politics of integration in England' in BARTON, L. and TOMLINSON, S. (eds) *Special Education and Social Interests*, London, Croom Helm.

BOYD KJELLEN, G. (1991) 'The "Kurator" system in Denmark' in *Disabled Youth: from school to work*, Paris, OECD.

BRADLEY, J. (ed.) (1985) *From Coping to Confidence*, London, FEU/NFER/DES.

BRADLEY, J. and HEGARTY, S. (1981) *Students with Special Needs in FE*, London, FEU.

BRENCHLEY, J. (1991) 'Muddling to the millennium', *Times Educational Supplement*, 5 July 1991, p. 16.

COOPER, D. (1988) *A Preparation for Adult Life: TVEI and special educational needs*, London, Skill.

CORBETT, J. (1989a) 'The quality of life in the "independence" curriculum', *Disability, Handicap and Society*, **4**(2), pp. 145–64.

CORBETT, J. (1989b) 'Bridging the sixteen-plus: a study of special school/college links', *Educare*, **34**, pp. 3–8.

CORBETT, J. (1990a) 'It's almost like work: a study of a YTS workshop', in CORBETT, J. (ed.) *Uneasy Transitions: disaffection in post-compulsory education and training*, Lewes, Falmer Press.

CORBETT, J. (1990b) *No Longer Enough: curriculum development in special school/college link courses*, London, Skill/Training Agency.

CORBETT, J. (1991a) 'Moving on: training for community living', *Educare*, **39**, pp. 16–18.

CORBETT, J. (1991b) *Reflections on Training Programmes by Trainees* (unpublished report for the Further Education Unit).

DEE, L. (1988) *New Directions*, London, FEU/NFER.

DEPARTMENT OF EDUCATION AND SCIENCE (DES) (1978) *Special Educational Needs*, Report of the Committee of Enquiry into the Education of Handicapped Children and Young People, London, HMSO (the Warnock Report).

DEPARTMENT OF EDUCATION AND SCIENCE (DES) (1982) *Statistical Bulletin 8/82, Additional Educational Needs*, London, HMSO.

DEPARTMENT OF EDUCATION AND SCIENCE (DES) (1984) *Report by HM Inspectors on Educational Provision and Response in some Haringey Schools*, London, HMSO.

DEPARTMENT OF EDUCATION AND SCIENCE (DES) (1985) *Better Schools*, London, HMSO.

DEPARTMENT OF EDUCATION AND SCIENCE (DES) (1991) *Education and Training for the 21st Century*, London, HMSO.

FARADAY, S. and HARRIS, R. (1989) *Learning Support*, Sheffield, Training Agency/Skill/FEU.

FENTON, M. and HUGHES, P. (1989) *Passivity to Empowerment*, London, Royal Association for Disability and Rehabilitation (RADAR).

FIRTH, H. and RAPLEY, M. (1990) *From Acquaintance to Friendship*, Kidderminster, British Institute of Mental Handicap.

FURTHER EDUCATION UNIT (FEU) (1989) *Towards a Framework for Curriculum Entitlement*, London, FEU.

GRIFFITHS, M. (1989) *Enabled to Work: support into employment for young people with disabilities*, London, FEU.

HACKETT, G. (1990) 'Abigail defies the odds', *Times Educational Supplement*, 18 May 1990, p. A5.

HARRIES, W. (1990) 'Students with severe learning difficulties and social integration' in THE OPEN UNIVERSITY (1990) DO5 Part B/E877 Module 6 *Providing for Special Needs: policy and practice, Offprint Book 6*, Milton Keynes, The Open University.

HICKOX, M. and MOORE, R. (1990) 'TVEI, vocationalism and the crisis of liberal education' in FLUDE, M. and HAMMER, M. (eds) *The Education Reform Act 1988*, Lewes, Falmer Press.

HUTCHINSON, D. and TENNYSON, C. (1986) *Transition to Adulthood*, London, FEU.

HURST, A. (1990) 'Obstacles to overcome: higher education and disabled students' in CORBETT, J. (ed.) (1990) *Uneasy Transitions: disaffection in post-compulsory education and training*, Lewes, Falmer Press.

JACKSON, M. (1990) 'Eager to shake hands with a one-time pariah', *Times Educational Supplement*, 6 July 1990, p. 10.

KINGSHOTT, L. (1991) 'Coping with work away from the centre', *Notes and Quotes*, 1, p. 5, London, Skill.

LILLYSTONE, C. and SUMMERSON, L. (1987) *Compendium of Post 16 Education and Training in Residential Establishments for Handicapped Young People*, Trowbridge, Wiltshire County Council.

MATTHEWS, M. (1990) 'Industry moves into the curriculum', *British Journal of Special Education*, **17**(3), pp. 95–7.

MCLAUGHLIN, E. (1991) *Social Security and Community Care: the case of the invalid care allowance*, London, HMSO.

NATIONAL UNION OF TEACHERS (NUT) (1990) *Special Education and Post 16 Students*, London, NUT.

O'GRADY, C. (1990) *Integration Working*, London, CSIE.

THE OPEN UNIVERSITY (1990) DO5 Part B/E877 Module 6 *Providing for special needs: policy and practice*, Milton Keynes, The Open University.

PHILLIPS, M. (1991) 'Bigger holes means net loss', *Guardian*, 19 April 1991, p. 20.

SHILLING, C. (1990) *Schooling for Work in Capitalist Britain*, Lewes, Falmer Press.

SKILL (1991a) *Educational Reform Act 1988 and Special Educational Needs: implications for local education authorities and further education colleges in England and Wales – a checklist on progress*, London, Skill.

SKILL (1991b) *Education and Training for the 21st Century: Government White Paper*, London, Skill.

STOWELL, R. (1987) *Catching Up?*, London, National Bureau for Handicapped Students.

SUTCLIFFE, J. (1990) *Adults with Learning Difficulties: education for choice and empowerment*, Leicester, NIACE/Open University Press.

TIMES EDUCATIONAL SUPPLEMENT (TES) (1991) 'Afterthoughts which ignore new beginnings', *Times Educational Supplement*, 5 July 1991, p. 17.

TOMLINSON, S. (1981) 'The social construction of the ESN(M) child' in BARTON, L. and TOMLINSON, S. (eds) *Special Education: policy, practices and social issues*, London, Harper and Row.

WHEELER, D. (1990) 'Business and education: motivating the workforce' in CORBETT, J. (ed.) *Uneasy Transitions: disaffection in post-compulsory education and training*, Lewes, Falmer Press.

WILKINSON, A. (1990) 'Complicated lives: students with special educational needs in the inner city' in CORBETT, J. (ed.) *Uneasy Transitions: disaffection in post-compulsory education and training*, Lewes, Falmer Press.

WILLIAMS, M. (1991) 'Cyrus's pathway to success', *MENCAP News*, **11**, pp. 4–5.

ACKNOWLEDGEMENTS

Grateful acknowledgement is made to the following for permission to reproduce material in this unit:

Text

Hackett, G. (1990) 'Abigail defies the odds', *Times Educational Supplement*, 18 May 1990, © Times Newspapers Ltd 1990; Matthews, M. (1990) 'Industry moves into the curriculum', *British Journal of Special Education*, **17**(3), September 1990.

Photographs

Page 28: Rob Judges; *page 47*: Kenn Palmer; *pages 21, 24–5, 41 and 48*: Mike Levers.

E242: UNIT TITLES